LIGHTNING BOLT BOOKS™

Great Warships

Brianna Kaiser

Lerner Publications ◆ Minneapolis

Lerner Publications Company
An imprint of Lerner Publishing Group, Inc.
241 First Avenue North
Minneapolis, MN 55401 USA

For reading levels and more information, look up this title at www.lernerbooks.com.

Main body text set in Billy Infant Regular. Typeface provided by SparkType.

Editor: Nicole Berglund

Library of Congress Cataloging-in-Publication Data

Names: Kaiser, Brianna, 1996- author.
Title: Great warships / Brianna Kaiser.
Description: Minneapolis : Lerner Publications, [2025] | Series: Lightning bolt books—Mighty military vehicles | Includes bibliographical references and index. | Audience: Ages 6-9 | Audience: Grades 2-3 | Summary: "Warships let the navy navigate and fight in the water. Readers will find out about the different types of warships and the technology they use"—Provided by publisher.
Identifiers: LCCN 2023040581 (print) | LCCN 2023040582 (ebook) | ISBN 9798765626177 (library binding) | ISBN 9798765628966 (paperback) | ISBN 9798765635162 (epub)
Subjects: LCSH: Warships—Juvenile literature.
Classification: LCC V765 .K35 2025 (print) | LCC V765 (ebook) | DDC 359.83—dc23/eng/20230831

LC record available at https://lccn.loc.gov/2023040581
LC ebook record available at https://lccn.loc.gov/2023040582

Manufactured in the United States of America
1-1009909-51951-11/21/2023

Table of Contents

Time to Land

A large warship moves through the ocean. A crew member standing on the deck waves a hand as a signal.

A navy plane lands on the warship. People on the warship are ready for more planes to land or take off.

An F-35 Lightning II lands on an aircraft carrier.

Navies around the world use warships. They are built to be faster and stronger than other ships.

The *USS Independence* is an aircraft carrier.

Navies use warships to protect areas of water from enemies. Warships also protect land and people along coasts.

All Kinds of Warships

There are many kinds of warships. Battleships, aircraft carriers, submarines, and cruisers are warships.

Battleships are large and made of steel. They can carry big guns.

This is the *USS Iowa*. The US Navy last used battleships in war in the 1990s.

The US Navy has thousands of planes. These planes can land on and take off from aircraft carriers.

Fighter jets sit on the runway of an aircraft carrier.

A runway

Aircraft carriers have a flight deck, or runway, where planes land and take off. When planes are not being used, they are stored below deck.

Submarines are built with an inner and outer hull so they don't break under the water's pressure.

Submarines travel underwater. As they go deeper, the weight of the water above increases the pressure on them.

Submarines have sonar. It uses sound waves to find other ships. Navy crew can use sonar to track enemies.

A crew member works in a control room.

A torpedo

Submarines also have a room to store weapons such as torpedoes. A torpedo is a kind of missile that travels through the water.

A cruiser

Cruisers are ships made
to travel with other ships.
Cruisers help guard or move
the ships around enemies.

Many Jobs

Navies use warships for lots of jobs. Warships can transport weapons, planes, and people.

These warships are lining up to form a blockade.

A navy might use a blockade to stop enemies from going in or out of a place. Blockades also stop people from moving items. Navies can use warships to create a blockade.

Navies can also use warships to protect ships that aren't used by the military.

Rescuing people is another use for warships.

Navies are always working to make warships better. What changes would you want to see on a warship? How else could people use warships?

Vehicle Diagram

USS Porter (DDG 78)

mast

weapons

hull

Fun Facts

- The first warships may have been built in Egypt five thousand years ago.

- The US Navy's TOPGUN program trains pilots.

- A group of warships is an armada.

Glossary

aircraft: any vehicle that can travel in the air

blockade: a barrier

navy: the part of a military that is based on the ocean

pressure: a strong force on a person or thing

signal: a way of sharing information

sonar: tech that finds the location of objects underwater

transport: to move or carry something from one place to another

Learn More

Billings, Tanner. *The U.S. Navy.* New York: Rosen, 2022.

Britannica Kids: Navy
https://kids.britannica.com/kids/article/navy/353522

Humphrey, Natalie. *Amazing Aircraft Carriers.* New York: Gareth Stevens, 2023.

Kiddle: Aircraft Carrier Facts for Kids
https://kids.kiddle.co/Aircraft_carrier

Kiddle: Warship Facts for Kids
https://kids.kiddle.co/Warship

Miller, Marie-Therese. *Strong Submarines.* Minneapolis: Lerner Publications, 2025.

Index

Photo Acknowledgments

Images used: U.S. Navy photo by Petty Officer 3rd Class Scott Pittman, p. 4; U.S. Marine Corps photo by Cpl. Thor Larson, pp. 5, 10; U.S. Navy photo by LTJG Caroline Hutcheson, p. 6; U.S. Navy photos provided by Navy Media Content Services, p. 7; U.S. Navy photo by Mass Communication Specialist 3rd Class Kurtis A. Hatcher, p. 8; U.S. Navy photo by Mass Communications Specialist 1st Class Eli J. Medellin, p. 9; U.S. Navy photo by Mass Communication Specialist Seaman Apprentice Karolina A. Martinez, p. 11; © U.S. Air Force photo by Tech Sgt. Westin Warburton, p. 12; U.S. Navy photos provided by Navy Visual News Service, Washington, D.C., p. 13; U.S. Navy photo by Mass Communication Specialist 2nd Class Michael H. Lee, p. 14; U.S. Navy photo by Mass Communication Specialist Seaman Apprentice Karolina A. Martinez, p. 15; U.S. Navy photo by Navy Visual News Service, p. 16; U.S. Navy photo by Jim Gibson, p. 17; U.S. Navy photo by Mass Communication Specialist 2nd Class Joshua Fulton, p. 18; U.S. Navy photo by Mass Communication Specialist 1st Class Michael B. Zingaro, p. 19; U.S. Navy photo by Mass Communication Specialist 2nd Class Nick Scott, p. 20.

Cover: U.S. Navy photo by Mineman 2nd Class Justin Hovarter.